for Eleanor and Glen,

With warm memories of
many great numbers of times.
(Eleanor — at least — now understands
my odd use of numbers.)

for
Lorraine
16 April 1964

The Wheel of Summer

for my two families:
*the one in which I was a child
and the one in which I have children*

The Wheel of Summer

by

Joseph Langland

THE DIAL PRESS   NEW YORK   1963

ACKNOWLEDGMENTS

"Willows," "A Little Homily," "Ecclesiastes," "The Serpent," "Dry Grass," "A Sea Change: For Harold," "Market Street Elementary Schook," "Winter Juniper," "War," "Henry Matisse," "Fall of Icarus: Brueghel," "Hunters in the Snow: Breughel," "Evergreen" are reprinted with the permission of Charles Scribner's Sons from *The Green Town* by Joseph Langland (*Poets of Today* III). Copyright 1944, 1951, 1953, 1954, 1955 Joseph Langland.

"A Sea Change: For Harold," "Evergreen," "Crane" and "Sacrifice of a Red Squirrel" were first published in *The New Yorker*.

Some of the poems in this volume were first published in magazines or anthologies as follows:

Accent, Listen (England), *London Magazine, The Nation, The New Mexico Quarterly, New Orleans Poetry Journal, New World Writing, The New Yorker, The Paris Review, Perspective, Poetry* (Chicago), *Poetry Northwest, Prism* (Canada), *Western Humanities Review, The Massachusetts Review, The Virginia Quarterly Review, The Northwest Review, The Saturday Review, Shenandoah,* the thirteen poem, pp. 96-119, appeared in *Poets of Today III.*

DESIGNED BY ALAN HEICKLEN

MANUFACTURED IN THE UNITED STATES OF AMERICA

BY THE HADDON CRAFTSMEN, INC., SCRANTON, PA.

CONTENTS

Sacrifices

Equations

Poems from *The Green Town*

Sacrifices

Haruspicating on Valley-View Farm

Sacrifice of a Rainbow Trout

Suddenly, from the rocky spring
A trout hung, trembling, in the air,
A jewel to the morning sun;

And then upon the mossy banks,
Rainy with rainbows, up he leaped
And tumbled wildly in the grass.

I ran to catch him where my hook
Pinned him behind a crusted rock
And ripped his mouth and gills apart.

I pulled his foaming stomach clean
And washed my fingers in the spring
And sat down and admired him.

His sunlit scales upon my hands,
I wrapped his flesh in leaves of elm
And homeward, singing, carried him.

I stripped him of his ivory bones,
Then held him, shining, to the fire
And tongued his body to my own.

And that was the supper that I had
While my imagination fed
Its silver hook upon the world.

Sacrifice of My Lamb

I broke from the womb of my mother
  and ran up the early years
Until on the cliffs of seven,
  with the gospel of senses scrying
The sun-flooded woodlands and valley,
  I came with confusions of tears
Under three black hawks to my pet,
  my baby-warm bottle lamb, dying.

He was torn with claws of his hanging,
  talons ripping the soft wreck
Of his body anointed with blood.
  I found his eyelids sinking
On curious sleep. Oh, then
  I awoke! I fell on his neck
And confounded the bleeding rose
  of my early innocence, shrinking.

I ran from his claw-slit belly;
  I ran from the pinkest prime
Incredible entrails dragged
  in dust of the limestone cliff.
I cried the nudge of his young bleats,
  puffing his sides at nighttime.
I ran to his tenderness once;
  now I left him, awkward and stiff.

I ran from the tree and shade
  of the juniper boughs where he lay;

I ran from the three dark wings,
           still trapped in the shades of stones,
And I lay in the leaves of the earth
           for a blasphemous long Sunday.
At last, when I saw him again,
           it was only to bury his bones.

I dug an abstraction of grave
           in erosions of one small head
And let that late wooly angel
           down, while some ghost said, bow!
And still I am wandering home,
           young seer gone blind in those dead
Miseries, crying, "God,
           God, where are your mercies now?"

Sacrifice of the Golden Owl

We strung our Wyandotte rooster, dead, on a post
And wired him fast, head up, white wings outspread
Just under the woodchuck trap. Then went to bed.

All night those great jaws looking at the sky
Above the swollen eyeballs of our cock
Waited for morning. But nothing made them lock.

Whatever it was that fed upon our world
Delayed his visiting, or else mistook
Those puffed red wattles with too close a look.

We thought it was some talon out of heaven,
Some claw-hook of the sky, some steel-hooked beak
With which we hoped our woodchuck trap would speak.

At last it did. Diving at striking noon,
A golden owl spilled downward like a sun,
Split my blue sky, and with the trap was one.

The feathered chain sang out and jerked until
I whacked his twisting head against that post.
He flopped, then ebbed, and dangled with his ghost.

I took him to the woodshed, sprang my knife,
And slit the shining golden breast apart,
Only to find a miserably small heart.

Then father cried, "Go take the rooster down."
I burned him with the trash, then ran and stood
The owl's heart on my new-split kindling wood.

I made a little ritual of that fire
To warm my heart, but wept above that breath
Singeing the tough cold bitterness of death,

And choked on the foulest odors of his wings
While all that dazzling plumage fanned upon
The plundered underworld which we had won.

Sacrifice of My Dog, Rex

When my dog came whimpering out of the hayfields,
Home from the mower's flickering sickle,
He lay on the floor of the fragrant haybarn
With the bleeding stub of the foreleg quivering,
The pool of convulsive death surrounding
      His white submissive eyes.

I heard him shout when he flushed a rabbit
In the honeyed webs of red-white clover.
I caught the quarry on quarry flashing.
He'll get him, I sang, and then it got him.
I froze where I stood, till his dark blood, flowing,
      Ran like a sword at my side.

He drank his wound, but that solemn supper
Gagged in his throat, and the tongue of comfort
Lay from his mouth. I had pulled a thorn from
The new-lost paw when I saw him suffer.
I had kissed that foot and washed and anointed
      Him under my whispered care.

And now it was lost in the fragrant hayfields
Where I ran out the honey of days in the clover;
And now he was going, that country greying
Under the edge of his eyes. Not knowing
Where then, or why, my small steps pointed
      The trail of his blood with prayers.

They stumbled his death to his life for meaning,
Winding across the yard and the roadway,
Out to the grainfield and into the hayfield,
Until, somewhere, they were lost forever
In a crown of sun and a field of flowers,
    And the ravenous sickle, reaping.

Sacrifice of The Old Gentleman

When our two great herd sires fought in the burroak grove
Their bellows disturbed my sleep. I rolled in a heat
Of black hooves stomping the bottomlands, woke in a sweat,

Crying, "Mother, what is it?" Father and brothers were gone.
"I'm afraid," she said, "that our sires have broken out long
Ago in the night. Oh, I hope that nothing is wrong."

Our great Hereford bulls! Their fierce heads were as strong
As the iron bars of their gates, their bodies as thickly
Bound as the earth they stormed. I ran off quickly.

My father with bullwhip and gun, my brothers in boughs,
And I on a limb above them, all up in the oak,
Stared a short ways off. Their deep growls broke

And sank in a tunnel of throat. The foam-bloodied nose
Of one bull hung from his curls on a forehead of hot
Dust. And his loud dull eyes, bleared cannon shot,

Fell on the other's entrails, trampled in leaves.
There the Old Gentleman, Prince Bill, Second, The Great,
Growled his proud way toward death, his enormous weight

Plunged to the ground he had stalked and pawed and shook.
The horn wound in his side was the single eye
With which my brothers and I could watch him die.

10

It took both tractors and the neighbor's chains,
Ringing the country stones, to pull him down
Into that ditch where those awful weeds have grown.

His calves were gentle, and the cows he rode
Became more gentle. Still, his awesome head
Arose on the horns of war. Now he is dead.

He shook his anger and iron sex in a wreath
Of forehead curls. But when his deep-tongued breath
Exploded, he charged the trembling woods with death

And so located, stalking before his grave,
Dimensions of himself. Now, scrawny and weak,
Our crows and mourning doves and coyotes speak

Those tired themes which none of us escape.
Sighs, croaks, and howls beset our greatest voice
With common years of indiscriminate noise.

Sacrifice of My Pet Chick

I combed his downy tail
Until chick drooped with love
And stepped, a peeping shame,
Into a boy's sad grave.

With water in my palm,
Small barley on my thumb,
I tucked his evening down
And broke his morning dream.

My cap his daily croft,
His wings atilt my head,
I strode through our barnyard
Among all winged men.

I wrapped his bobbing head
In frayed tails of my shirt;
I strung his strawy web
With weed stalks for a perch.

At last, he only sat;
And then, he only lay.
And afterwards I had
Him ten days from the grave.

An earthworm filled his eyes;
Some ants cleaned out his skull.
Two beetles on his thigh
Were scarcely beautiful,

So I scraped those tiny bones.
They broke. His awful wings
Lie, for all I have known,
Still bleaching under the sun.

Sacrifice af My Neighbors

Wonder at the world's madness!
      Then tell your heart
To toll most tenderly, and toss
In a kind of comic sadness
While we count our neighbor losses, part by part.
There is no loss until the final loss.

One lost his hand in a corn-shredder,
      The clockwork claws
Striking with anonymity,
Measuring space before them
Beyond the saving speculative pause,
Surprising him, and still amazing me.

One lost his toe in a woodpile,
      The indifferent axe
Pursuing the arc of the driven arm
Beyond the dry wood, splitting,
Having no mind for what its body lacks,
Steel head on wood, adjudicating harm.

One lost his arm in a flywheel;
      The gasoline belt
Wrenched and ripped, stuttered and ran,
To grind the grain in the cornmill.
And that rude noise said what it had not felt
In that rude juncture for the assistant, man.

One lost his right leg under
      A tractor's rim,

Muscle and bone dissenting there
In a circular steel tremor;
Invading him, it made discrete in him
That symbol of the body's messenger.

One lost his child in flood waters
　　　　When walls of rain
Collapsed on neighboring hills and streamed
Over the valley pastures.
He had not read the clouds as an ocean plain
Until the water crashed our hearts and screamed.

One lost his mind to his childhood.
　　　　We saw those dumb
Erosions backward from that shore
Where we had lately known him,
Being as strong and handsome as they come.
Now he is scarcely two-three years or more.

One lost his love to a madman
　　　　Who sped through night
With pistol and teeth flashing and went
Down with her death in the morning,
A darkness upon darkness, even in light,
Since no one who kept his mind guessed what it meant.

One lost his heart to a mender
　　　　Who trembled his hope.
Oh Jesus, the miracles of men
Are blind in that great valley
Where time engages the eternal slope,
And once run down may not be wound again.

And I lost my fear in these losses.
　　　　Though they carouse
Stealthily with my neighbors, still
Many are not failing,
And I am surely walking in that house
Where mind will not, though all my body will.

Sacrifice of My Young Mare,
Great with Colt

The blue guts of the evening
Spilled from the belly of God,
As I walked alone with my father
Across our grassy valley
And into the muddy bottoms.

Almost beyond believing,
A mudhole rimmed with rocks
Had swallowed our colt-great filly
Up to her bloated belly.
They swam together, rotting.

She was still alive, but heaving,
Choked in her muddy cud,
And I cried to my father, "Father,
What can we do?" "No telling.
Now she's going. We've lost one."

No rope or machine extending,
No stay of her heart or blood,
No hand outreached with power
Could help, or could even rally
The blasted day we were caught in.

I stood on that edge, deceiving
Myself that the swollen pod
Could spill itself in the quick-mud
And walk from our grassy valley
To the upland hills and the barn.

But her muddy death, upcreeping,
Swallowed the blood of her womb;
It crept on her foam-wet withers,
The bursting head overwhelming.
Then the last white eye, exploding,

Slipped under, beyond all seeing.
Caught there, in the belly of God
As I stood alone with my father,
I saw the blood of the mother
Bubble the pots of death.

They broke in dark circles, pleading
Completion in me. Unhoused,
The dark gods stood in the thickets.
My father said nothing. Aching,
I climbed the old slope toward home.

Sacrifice of A Gunnysack of Cats

The quick small bubbles popping from the gunnysack,
Hooked by a pitchfork braced in the cattle tank,
Almost unhinged my heart and made me drop
The stick with which I forced the young cats down.

A population explosion, that's what it was.
With twelve mother cats and a year of visiting toms
We met September with the wildest host
Of squinting eyes behind our milking cows.

We divvied them up among the brothers and sisters,
And each had only six. But since we were nine
My father thought things were getting out of hand.
Next day I received my melancholy orders.

"You'll have to catch the most of them and drown them.
Just tidy up the place and make it normal.
Fifty-four cats! Why, that's an infernal nuisance.
Think what would happen next year!" What could I tell him?

So there I was dashing with my gunnysack
Into the bins and under the stalls and mangers.
The wild ones scratched me, but I thrust them in.
The tame ones? Oh, I brushed them with my cheek,

Sighed and kissed them, then I thrust them in.
I climbed the ladders to the highest mows,
Ran through the orchard under the heavy apples
And crept among the tall weeds by the granary,

Until I thought I could not bear that cross.
I dropped it once; that made it twice as hard
To lure them once again into that womb
And bear it backward to the spermal waters.

But there I was: filthy, bleeding, and sick,
Tired and thirsty, my cord pulled at its neck,
The undulating coffin on my waggon,
Trudging down to the sea, my cross upon me.

The thorny dissonance of dying song
Over the squealing of the wagon wheels
Ran up a cloud of dust that nearly drowned me.
It is one thing to think, and one to do.

I wanted to avoid the thinking in the doing
And, quick, be done with it and off to play.
But you can see this didn't work too well . . .
Thirty-three years to get that cord untied.

I stood in the dust manure at my feet,
The green scum in the corners of the tank
Eyeing my smothering conscience toward a size
My body could not hold. Good God, I seized

That squirming sepulchre, that crying tomb,
That leaping heart familiar as myself,
And heaved it from my homemade hearse and plunged
It back to evolution. Hooking the fork,

I ticked five awful minutes by the hours,
Damned by the furious bubbles where they broke
Among my unwashed hands. And then I went
Up to the barn to find my mother cat.

We sat in a beam of sunlight on the floor
Petting and purring, while out of a knothole eye
Hung in the roof of God the motes of dust
Sang of our comforts and our curious loves.

Sacrifice of A Rattlesnake

No one was looking, but the fat
Female rattlesnake had just curled on an edge of sun
Around the shade of a rockpile in the pasture.

Under her white white belly (down, keep down!)
Ovals and triangles of brown-white and grey stones
Broke in irregular sharp patterns from her scaly back.

Such shameful camouflage invests our dust.

Maybe the eye of God (but nothing else)
Was watching her wary slumbers by the springs
Where we played the daylong summer out,
Barefoot in overalls.

We shouted out of the grass
And splashed up out of the springs,
Swishing over those rocks.
She rattled and leapt and struck.

Then everyone came running.

We pinned her head with a stick.
We bashed her body.
We cracked her tail.
We squashed her head with rocks.
We tumbled the white eye of her body up
And slashed it with the knife-edge of our fear,
Only to see,

Descending from that wound,
Three tiny snakes
Slipping in shadowed crevices of rocks
To flick the old relentless eye of God.

Sacrifice of The Old Sow

They said she was wild when the old sow ate the pigs
She farrowed into her straw in the stock-warm barn
Early in March. I caught her crunching the last
One in her jaws, then clung to the filthy patched
Gate and swallowed my breaking new-born tears.

My brother rushed at the sow, "You goddamn bitch,"
Jabbing his pitchfork in the bloodmother's flank;
"You devil, you goddamn devil," my brother screamed,
Trumpeting all the four ends of her pen
Wherever she crashed, "You bitch, you goddamn bitch."

I squeezed my eyes again at the rawest noise
Flung like manure on the squealing boards.
How could I know, my small hands to my heart,
That this huge barn-of-a-world was also stuffed
By Darwin and Marx and Freud at the feeding troughs?

And so, at last, there were only a hundred and twelve
Pigs to be raised. And since the old sow had fed
On the offspring she conceived, we strung her up
And slit her throat and stripped her down and ate
That succulent rib with which we kept alive.

Sacrifice of My Cousin

Such violence was uncalled for.
Inside the furnace jacket,
Clear in summer, my cousin struck a match,
Provident long before his winter came.
    And down it blew at once,
    All blaze and infernal racket.

How he came up, not even
His God, the Father, is telling,
But up he came without his hair and clothes
In such disasters that even to mention shame
    Were simply to take another
    Subject for all our knelling.

Such shocking news defended
But few of our family blessings.
Though we had heard of a furnace and its hot breath
No one had had such an agent before his death,
    And why it should now appear
    Is not even among our guessings.

We hold such a little space,
This more or less to our measure,
And some few friends, both more or less to our taste.
Now my dear cousin is dead, in that rude waste
    I must honor the flame in us all,
    The warmth of our daily pleasure.

Sacrifice of a Flock of Sheep

The dogs broke up our sheep in the lambing time of the year;
Out the wild woods they fled to limestone bluffs, pell-mell,
And over the cliff they went, the whole flock mad with fear.

They felt the springing pain of the bursting month was near,
And dumbly they saw themselves caught up in the general
     swell,
But dogs broke up our sheep in the lambing time of the year.

All that the white domestic and heavy ewes would hear
Upon any April evening was the tinkling low sheep bell,
But over the cliff they went, the whole flock mad with fear.

Eyes and bleats were mild, and they stepped daintily here
As though they trusted masters. They trusted them too well,
And dogs broke up our sheep in the lambing time of the year.

What maddens gentle natures? What made them wildly steer
Into the upper woodlands? Who caught them in his spell?
Over the cliff they went, the whole flock mad with fear.

There they lie with their wombs in the double death we fear
Where time and occasion take a toll we can scarcely tell;
The dogs broke up our sheep in the lambing time of the year,
And over the cliff they went, the whole flock mad with fear.

Sacrifice of Uncle Hans

He kept the fires and dusted the sacristy
And rang the countryside to worship Sundays.
He watered graves and even dusted tombstones.
I don't know what-in-the-world he did on Mondays.
    (People generally laughed
      when they mentioned Uncle Hans.)

He lounged outside the men's room Sunday evenings,
Social with punks who wanted to be social
And still not too religious. He bowed goodnight
To the last host, and part of the week he rested.
    (How much of the week, I wondered,
      when I thought of Uncle Hans.)

He never married, but he kept one cow,
A couple of goats, litter of pigs, some trapgear,
Some whiskey for when the church got cold and lonely,
And a spry brace of horses he drove everywhere.
    (My, what a time we planned,
      waiting for Uncle Hans.)

He came to clear the downlogs from our timber
One winter in his sleigh; he looked so rosy
My brother said he must have nipped his whiskey
And swallowed half the bottle when he broke her.
    (Even those who disapproved
      allowed that to Uncle Hans.)

He came with sleighbells ringing in the roadways
And went with laughter bouncing in us children,
Until my father cut the rope that bore him
Off to the graveyard he had kept so tidy.
>   (No use in laughing, then,
>   when they mentioned Uncle Hans.)

When the bells rang, Old Hans was in the tower,
And all the ladies' socials on the lawns
Were placed there by his hands. My, off he went,
And no one put a stone where he had gone.
>   (Most of the stones I knew
>   were set by Uncle Hans.)

Our weekly confidence held no account
With such extravagance of early rest;
So the local mortuary took his litter
Of pigs, goats, and cow, and did their best.
>   (No one ever seemed to do
>   as well as Uncle Hans.)

But I saw Old Hans hanging from his shed beams,
Dangling beyond the lantern light that found him,
And lying beyond the scripture that we read him.
Some think it isn't so, but he sleeps soundly.
>   (St. Paul and the others tried,
>   but they didn't know Uncle Hans.)

He had a heart, well, more than he could afford.
If many things he did didn't seem quite right,
You knew he was always giving, if you kept any score.
And Lord, how jolly! Well, let him sleep for a while.
>   (I'll not say any more, now;
>   you see, I loved Uncle Hans.)

Except that I've got to add that when he was hanging,
Purpled and swollen with scorn, nothing we knew
From prophets to Plato to psalms and Luther and back
Seemed of much use. But I won't let memory go.
(It's the best good thing we have.
I remember my Uncle Hans.)

Sacrifice of The Sparrows of the Field

My mother and sisters washed out each other's
Hair in sweet lemons and purest rainwaters;
And so did the neighboring girls and their mothers,
Lounging on porchswings on long summer mornings.
    Whenever the rain fell
    They ran with pails full
    Of water from eavespouts
    Pouring in cisterns.
When I dribbled a milkwhitened pebble downward
Into the softwater well depth, it whispered
In circles of girlfaces, wreathed and laughing;
Maybe it didn't, and maybe it mattered.
    But sparrows clogging
    The eavetroughs hanging
    Under our houses
    Were clouding our waters.
Horse hair and barn straw and cow dung together
They wove into cozy egg homes as they twittered,
And downy cock feathers in scissor-beaks shredded,
With mosses and mudroots packed in for filler.
    Dark summer showers
    And spouting baubles
    Broke from our shingles
    On sisters and mothers.
Whenever straight hair hung stringy and oily
My father and brothers were cursing the sparrows,
And up in the rain went the twin-sliding ladders,
And down came the baby sparrows, splashing.

28

Naked wet sorrows,
Babes in my palms, then,
Bled out of tenderness.
Dying becalmed them.
God knew that they clogged the troughs with odd odors
And, filthy with lice from their barnridden feathers,
Strained to our wells. Then sisters' and mothers'
Hair hung unwashed on their breasts and their shoulders.
For whatever is hanging—
Angel or evil—
Over our eyelids,
God must be answering.
In a crown of sweet Sundays, their services psalming
In wreaths of hair-presses and redolent showers,
Golden and brown under summerlace bonnets,
The rainwater mothers and sisters are singing
Bird-warbled summer
And rain-washed dripping
In cisterns drumming.
Bless the sweet sinner,
But our fine rural ladies must wash in rainwater.
We climb in our world, all brothers and fathers,
And run where it bells us, attacking and loving,
To sing the pure Sunday of sisters and mothers.

And sleep out the years in the arms of our lovers.

Sacrifice of Gophers and Woodchucks

When I was a young one
I used to trap gophers
(10¢ for the ears, and 15¢ for the hide)
And caught woodchucks.
It was all business pride;
Nobody stung one.

I got up at five—
I mean, really early—
(10¢ for the ears, and 15¢ for the hide)
And jangled my traps
At my shoulder sides;
Man, I was alive.

I carried a stick-club
In my right hand, always
(10¢ for the ears, and 15¢ for the hide).
It was all you needed
To finish them off with:
A quick sharp thud.

Gophers brought thistles.
That's what neighbors said
(10¢ for the ears, and 15¢ for the hide).
They ruined the grainfields,
The whole countryside.
Had sharp whistles.

Pa didn't like them.
Neither did I

(10¢ for the ears, and 15¢ for the hide).
    If he had a pitchfork
    By when I caught one,
    Quick, he'd spike him.

    When taut chains drag
    In a woodchuck's hole
(10¢ for the ears, and 15¢ for the hide).
    You know, if it goes
    All slack on the guide,
    She bit off a leg.

    Easy, I pulled them
    Home from their burrows
(10¢ for the ears, and 15¢ for the hide);
    Then's when I slugged them.
    It saved my pride
    For when I sold them.

    Inflation caught me
    By my confirmation
(10¢ for the ears, and 15¢ for the hide).
    It seems that I never
    Will keep my pride
    With what that brought me.

    But I like looking back
    On those natural hours
(10¢ for the ears, and 15¢ for the hide),
    Barefoot at dawn
    With chucks on the hills,
    Fresh ears in my sack.

    This is not hearsay.
    I've been a young trapper
(10¢ for the ears, and 15¢ for the hide),
    And I'm not surprised seeing
    Some people at morning
    Crying, "God a mercy!"

Sacrifice of The Grey Wolf

Trotting in wintry rounds of bleak intent,
He hung upon the distant knolls and draws
As if he sought each one of us, alone,
Howling our very names. Our heads were bent
Sidewise to hear him wail against our cause.
We gouged his tracks, losing him. Then he was gone.

He should have kept his nature to himself,
But no, he let it fray the winter air
And trail along the bottomlands of sleep
In vague drifts. One night the limestone shelf
Announced him from a cave we came to share.
Another night, he rode among the deep

Thicketed hills and gnashed our dreams apart.
Next came his southeast wail. Next night the north
Wildlike area under the close ravine
Sprang at the chill of dawn and froze our heart.
At last, we knew a hunter must go forth
To be hunted while he hunted. The icy sheen

Upon the crusts of snow broke underfoot
And sifted downward through the winter's flight.
Morning and evening stood in equal wait
Upon the house of sleep, zeroed and mute.
And when the stars sang out upon the night
His shadow flashed beyond our barnyard gate.

We heard the westward wailing of the winds
Under that threat, or over it. Who knew?
Shivering, we waited it out upon the stark
Echoes of grey disaster, while our minds
Hobbled the sheepyards with the crippled ewe.
My sisters woke up screaming in the dark.

Wake, wake up, we whispered. It's a dream, but tell.
And out of sleep-knotted hair their eyes still saw
What young mouths mumbled, as if it came to pass.
His tongue was an ashen grey where the comet fell.
His tooth was an edge of world. His enormous jaw
Was the old abyss. And his claws were shattered glass.

Then up it stood, the manlike beast to the child.
The audible prophecies rippled under its throat
And growled in the flowery gardens of their youth,
Prowling their flannel comfort. Beyond those wild
Peripheries of warmth the occasions gloat,
Skirting our fairy woods with a grey truth.

Who howls at midnight from the bottomlands,
Degrading us with watching, while the gun
Stands with its polished eye inside the hall?
Who cocked the safety for uneasy hands?
Run to the north ravine. Who hides? We run.
We aim, we stand, we wait. Is it nothing, at all?

Had the sly fiend but slashed across our gate
And sunk his teeth into the heifer's shanks,
Or ripped our ram to death, and dripping, fled,
We could have settled then. But that grey fate
Wasted our rest behind the bloodiest flanks
Of frayed imaginations in our head.

A stutter out of the henhouse late at night,
And all our nerves went cackling up on edge
Until the cock-mad mornings struck them off.
A bleat among our breathings, and the light
Flickered the lamps and waved the bedroom walls
With ghostly nightgowns under the winter's cough.

Out of the west, then out of the east, he comes.
He rattles corn-shocked fields and shadows huts
Of blackberry patches prickling under the snow.
We riffle our winter buttons, shaking, all thumbs,
And batter our wits and jab our fists in our guts.
For God's sake, take what you want! Take it and go.

He took it, but early next spring in the gorged ravine
His fur made ragged patches along the ground,
And his belly was split and stinking upon the fence.
And there the old shadows flickered over the scene
Until we stood, with the circling days, around
The sunburst of our vast indifference.

There the nights walking at the grey wolf's side
Stole out below the morning's upper rim
Under the spring upleaping in the wood;
And there we all live, where none of us can hide.
I even think I'll be expecting him
From the dark winters talking in our blood.

Sacrifice of Three Wild Geese

Three geese blew down the wintry air.
    Some law condemned their cries
And did them in. I saw the snow
    Drift on their bloodshot eyes.

Native to God, they whacked our stream
    And flopped on solid ice,
Scrying our blasted hills with errant
    Instincts of advice.

All homing prophecies of spring
    Were glazed with glassy spears;
Our granaries, at zero blue,
    Were buttoned to their ears.

Three geese, shucks! The silly birds,
    Who taught them to repeat
Unseasonable Indian-summer tales,
    Our climate of deceit?

History warned us farmers. We
    Put up the corn; we drove
Our cattle near the barns; we split
    Huge woodpiles for the stove.

Down went our trees and down our grain;
    Down went our windows, down
Our butchered steers, our blooded lambs,
    And all our roots went down.

We packed our house against the ice,
    Our food below the storm;
Carnivorous, we fed on death
    And kept our bodies warm

And rode the bitterest winter out
    Until the larks and wrens
Came walking up the April clouds
    And chatted with our hens.

Still, on the shortest Sundays, still
    Three alien images
Of death pursue me down the skies
    Past neighboring villages

And bear their tale upon my tongue
    Until the sunniest doubt
Wrings out the latter days of March
    And lays their history out.

Yet there they hover, angel-like,
    Annunciating wrong:
A rune, a legend of my own,
    And an old folk song.

Sacrifice of Eric

Missing our neighbor, we searched the empty sheds.
We called his name along the iced creek-beds.
Eric, we sang upon the rocky draws,
Eric, and then we faced the silent pause
With one ear cocked to the world.
                            Somehow, we knew,
But we kept pretense alive a day or two,
Following any tracks laid out in snow
Until we trailed ourselves in the moonglow.
And all that time, in woods by the gravel beds,
He stood in his swollen postures over our heads,
Hanging, frozen, and swinging free in air.
We stopped, a few feet off, too baffled there
To talk or move. Someone took off his hat.

Well, he was found. At least, we had done that.

Who got my neighbor there upon that limb?
        All those dark faces murmuring at his back?
Who slipped the latest noose that carried him?
        Did he? We looked; there was no other track.
Who quickened the thicket clutching at our clothes?
        Did he? The woodlands quaked upon our cries.
And who could read the winter's tale he knows?
        We saw that pale abyss, the unlidded eyes.
Who swung him out and downward from that bough?
        Did he? For fear our hanging hearts would break
We cut him down. Who bears his burden now?
        Who swings us all? Forbear, for Jesus' sake.

Toward those intolerable silences we came,
And action saved us when the mind was lame.
We tried some magic for an old complaint
And bowed.
              I thought some medieval saint
Stepped gently from the wounded wood which bore
Old Eric like a gargoyle evermore
And gave him, with eroded hands, a crown.

But seeing it wasn't so, we let him down
And carried him out across our bottomlands,
The deadweight of his world upon our hands,
And heard, and hear, in sudden solitudes,
An old wind walking in our lower woods.

I call him my own neighbor, when I dare,
But that's not easy, having come from there.

Sacrifice of a Red Squirrel

Leaping from oak to oak, tangled-up in the woods,
      Grey squirrels and reds
Scrambled in elegant furs with nuts in their heads.
That was their life; they didn't know any other.
      Spring, once arrayed
In sun-checkered flowers, stood in its climate of shade
      Crying,
    Squirrels, beware, beware;
      Red squirrel, run!
The fixed ideas are coming to hunt you down.

Three boys strolled up to the woods from neighboring farms
      With a twenty-two gun.
They wanted a red squirrel fur. Red squirrel, run!
That was their life. Why should they learn of another?
      Quick targets in trees
Were trophies of summer, red squirrels the rarest of these,
      Crying,
    Squirrels, beware, beware;
      Red squirrel, run!
The fixed ideas are coming to hunt you down.

Bang went the gun. Grey squirrels ran into their holes;
      And red squirrel now,
With his front leg flapping, clung to the uppermost bough
Quivering with life. If he would know of another
      Some instinct could hide
An eye of himself around on the opposite side,
      Crying,

Squirrels, beware, beware;
　　　Red squirrel, run!
The fixed ideas are coming to hunt you down.

Red was the sheen of his coat; then it glistened in sun
　　　Redder than red;
Teetering high on his claws, he chattered and bled
And hung to his home. How could he cling to another?
　　　Then up came a stone
And tickled the paw of the leg with the bullet-hung bone,
　　　Crying,
　　Squirrels, beware, beware;
　　　Red squirrel, run!
The fixed ideas are coming to hunt you down.

Then up came showers of stones and bangs from the gun,
　　　Shouts from the boys,
And the green home trembled over that chaos of noise.
Alive to this life, and not having known any other,
　　　Red squirrel, come down;
Crawl at their feet and ride in their sack to the town,
　　　Crying,
　　Squirrels, beware, beware;
　　　Red squirrel, run!
The fixed ideas are coming to hunt you down.

And now in their halls he hangs on a missile of skins,
　　　While mere boys comb
The wing-diving furs that flew in the airiest home.
And that is their life; they still do not know any other.
　　　Oh, wild riddled woods,
Autumnal with reds, quake in your great green hoods,
　　　And cry,
　　Squirrels, beware, beware;
　　　Red squirrel, run!
The fixed ideas are coming to hunt you down.

40

Sacrifice of a Hill of Ants

We gathered the winter wood in the middle of fall,
Working with brush fires going, meant for scraps
From trimming the trees of spindly twigs, and bark
Fallen in chips of timber from the axe.
This kept us tidy, and it kept us warm,
And though it wasted upward in a flash
Of crackling blaze too sudden for much good,
     At least, we knew it would.

That acrid smoke, mischievous in the wind,
Drove us off from a tree we had felled, and I,
Idling around with sparks, spied an ant hill
And red ants scurrying upwind from the fire.
I teased a little flame upon a stick,
Then bore it, flickering forward like a smile,
And stuck it in the middle of their run
     For a little harmless fun.

Snatching our spade, I thrust it at the top
Of that small hill and cast it to one side.
There an amazing city in all its crowd
Of rapid instincts, wrinkled in ruts of time,
Ran far beyond my innocence. Those dots
Danced to the sparkling missiles in their eyes,
So I submarined another underground
     To watch them run around.

The way they seized their wealth and hauled it off,
A frenzy of intention, I could tell

They knew where they were going, sure of forms;
Those bright corrupted arteries were shed
As if deliberate speed could save them all.
How could they know what I was up to next,
Arriving with a pitchfork filled with fire
      Upon their town entire?

In all their miniature wisdom suddenly trapped,
They ran off crazily for their cellar homes
Under such sunlight that their heads went mad
And twisted all the wits their world had known.
They buckled in bloom, rolled in a dead flash,
While odors from their parching bodies rose,
Nut-brown, below the cataclysmic pyres
      Of the afternoon's desires.

Then the wind shifted, so back we went to work.
Our young arms flailed upon October's ease
Toward oven breads and kitchen chairs all rocked
Back from the roaring stove on a winter's eve.
Chatting casually, snug in a chilly world,
We worked the pivot of fire, while a smoky dream
Rose from the miniature hill where a thousand heads
      Sang in their crackling beds.

Sacrifice of Aunt Marie

My anemic aunt was alone in her flower garden
(Roses, petunias, wealthies, foxcomb and phlox)
On a Fourth-of-July that always seems fragrant with bloom,
When all of her nephews crept from the north of her house
(Cherries and winesaps, spearmint and red four-o'clocks)
And threw their firearms round in a crackerjack boom.

None of us looked, but Oh with what brilliance we ran
(Jellies and jonathans, peppermint, lilacs and mums)
And perched on our naughtiest wits by the Bear Creek rocks
And laughed till the sun set. Then we went back to look
(Thornwood, bleeding hearts, bittersweet, currants and
        plums),
And three days later we lowered her down in a box.

The old ladies patted us gently upon our heads
(Laces and liniment, cosmos and hoarhounds and thyme)
Where we sat alone in the shade of her northernmost doors.
The old men nodded and slyly glanced at their clocks
(Oh, gardens of heartsease, rainbowing honey of time),
And when we grew up we all went off to the wars.

The Wheel of Summer

The dark land rose in the luminous arch of sky.
The bald sun softly grew. Down by the barn
My father and we three sons watched how it fell
Through hazes of sour dust by the old pig pens.
"They got away from us," my father said.
He didn't need to say it. The great sun god
Bowed to the grassy sea by the western hills,
Darkened to blood, rolled in the tasseled corn
And flamed our blinking eyeballs. "Yup," we said,
And turned in the dirty twilight to our thoughts.

    Those silken shoats with jiggling nuts
    Went squealing under their mothers' tits
    Two months too long, until they ran
    Smelling each other around the pens
    And snuffled into a herd of lusts.
    Ourselves but fifteen, fourteen, twelve,
    We knew that wrestling those young boars
    And bearing them, sterile, up from the knives
    With bristling feet and foaming mouths
    Could bend our steel and twist our smiles.

We ambled, loose in overalls, up by the house.
We doused our barny hands in sun-warmed waters,
Waited for supper, glanced at the girls, then ate.
We counted a few odd stars and the evening star
Over the glut of summer. Later, upstairs,
We stripped and gathered a pillow into our arms,
Rolled in the humid nightfall once or twice,
Muttered a thing or two, then fell asleep.

The women swept the kitchen,
Carried the washing waters,
Scrubbing towels and basins.
We slept. They quietly chatted,
Loosened their hair and spread it
In puffs for summer dreaming.

Out of those dreaming coves
The dawn broke, suddenly,
And rolled the milk-dust haze
Up Bekkan's Ridge. We yawned,
Straightened the slack in our mouths,
Tightened our muscles a notch,
Wrinkled our groins like a gourd,
And marched on out to the barn.

Then father called, "Let's drive them in."
We harried pigs toward the dusty barn,
Kicked the shoats and rammed the door
And banged the bar in its wooden home.
Coarse as our job, we whaled them all
Till some walked, upright, on the gates
And flowed together. "Wet them down!"
In the stock-tank our buckets swam,
Slipped and swished and, bellying up,
Went shivering over the slithering pens.
Our badgered strength was out of mind
In summer madness: a sty of sounds.

Our father, priest and teacher, led us on.
We stood in the sire's circle while he talked,
Whipped out his knife and whetted it on stone.
He flipped some acrid lysol from his jug
To test it out, then touched the slicing blade
Gingerly over his thumb. All set to go.
"Boys, let's bring them on." We'd bring them on.

We eyed the mob,
Curious, queasy.
Grey dust flowered
Under the rafters.
Breathy and muddy,
They surged together
In sour odors.

The three of us dove down the herd.
I grabbed one, dared not let him go.
Some boyish pride threw out my arms
To catch the unsuspecting world.
They clamped like iron. Crushing him,
I locked him to my chest and bore
Him, staggering, to the trough. Hair,
Plastered with dust, bristled my arms.
"Hup, flip him now!" Damned if I didn't,
But square on his feet. Off he ran,

His bony tail stretched outward from my hands,
He charged the herd. I hauled him down again,
And up from the pigsty floor we two arose,
Loudly embracing. And for what purposes?
"Hang on this time!" You think I would've lost him?
I knew when we were working, not at games,
When to be gentle, when to play it rough;
One cannot breed ten thousand animals
Into this world and woo them for the axe
Without a curse and prayer to help him through.

I got him upside down in the trough
And hung on his heels. I stomped his chest.
My brother locked his squealing snout.
With lysol, tender flesh was doused;
That knife dipped in the slickest stroke
I ever saw this side of hell,
And murderous music, like a crime,
Gurgled that milk-blue blooded dream.

46

Snip went the cords; the mindless body doubled.
Flick went the blade again; the shades of change
Rolled down the dust beyond the feeding troughs,
A tough abstraction. Dropping the crippled pig,
We rolled him out and ran him down the alley.
He walked so gingerly he seemed to dance
With quivering hooves upon the ragged straw
Along the barn. The solemn way he went,
He must have dumbly felt some ancient law
Driving him out of nature's benediction.

        Infected with truth,
        We hung in dust
        Drenched to our skins,
        Bleached to our bones.
        He sat in the straw
        Mute as a rock,
        Crudely undone.
        Ranker than swine,
        Coarse to our nails
        We swung to our job.

        Then we went all the way
        To common terms with loss.

        Having run down our guilt and pain,
        We lobbed the curses from our mouths.

We trapped them all. We never bore so much
Next to our hearts. We caught them with our feet,
Caged them for death and shrilled them back to life
To trot, untroubled, fattening for your grace.
So we prepared your table. The awful world
Seemed natural as breathing. Brazen with swine,
We hounded the living daylights out of the earth.
Nature we rolled, denatured, in the straw
Where loss waits in the alleys like a snake,

47

Coiled and ready, although it cannot strike.
The last lay down exhausted, wouldn't run.
We could have lain down with him. Had he fought
We might have, in our weakness, let him go.
At last, we spun the gates and turned them out
Under the burroak trees by the young alfalfa.
The barrows wandered through the blooming grasses.
We poured some water for their healing mudbaths.
We filled their troughs with generous sour mashes.
Burying snouts, they snuffled in rows of pigs' eyes,
And we, stinking high heaven, turned and trotted
Slowly along the woodpaths into the valley.

How shall I praise the valley waters,
The crystal springs so sweetly aching
Over our bruised, our lusty bodies?

We slid in water like sluggish wishes
And lay on sandbanks, mute and weary.
The water idled over our heartbeats.

We blew cool water out of our noses
With the clotted curses and gray mucus
And rose in our summer limbs for drying.

From sparkling stones we walked; then, dressing
In cleanest clothes on the polished gravels,
We stretched ourselves on yielding grasses,

While healing evening came.
We felt another dream
Rise in our flesh and feed
The mouth of mysteries;
It flickered in our minds
And quivered in our thighs.
Sweeping across our limbs,

48

It loosed our fumbling tongues
Until, at last, we talked
About the neighbor girls
And joked among ourselves.

We rose from the banks. For the evening star
Our casual wishes and shadowy groves
Welled with a tougher grace. To the barn
We rocked with the great maternal cows
And milked them down with our gentlest hands.

Next morning took us like an old surprise.
Fallen, with old corruption in our arms,
We praised the animal urgencies of love,
Our long obedience. The mind of man,
Boyishly wandering out of the eye of God,
Seemed natural to our wills. Our bruised bones
Took on this sweet admission. Proud in the sun,
Calloused and cocked, wicked and wise and young,
We ran, three golden idols, back to chores,
Shouldered the wheel of summer, and journeyed on.

Equations

Ballad of Poor Will

I was got with a cowlick, and so will I end,
    Sunlight and summer and sun,
My hair all awry, even into the grave,
        Into the grave,
And even there twisting. God, may you send,
    Starlight and autumn and rain,
Grimaces and psalmings to mull in my face,
    Washing and making me clean.

Burn all my blemishes, scattered and splotched,
    Sunlight and summer and sun;
They even unbalanced the wings of my brain,
        Wings of my brain.
If dust will accept them, wrinkled and botched,
    Starlight and autumn and rain,
It can slowly reject them. Let the years fail,
    Washing and making me clean.

For I had a birthmark, and I had a love,
    Sunlight and summer and sun,
One harsh on my neck and one soft in my arms,
        Soft in my arms,
One cold in my heart and one deep in the grove,
    Starlight and autumn and rain,
But I cherished the chill, and I wasted the warmth
    Washing and making me clean.

And I got a scar on my strong right thigh,
    Sunlight and summer and sun,

And a wart on my hand, some moles on my back,
                    Moles on my back,
And a wandering vein in the edge of my eye,
        Starlight and autumn and rain . . .
Oh, take me again to the old mummy sack,
        Washing and making me clean.

And I got a twitch in my left cheekbone,
        Sunlight and summer and sun,
Which a beggar would notice with scarcely a smile,
                  Scarcely a smile,
But crushed in my straw, and at night, and alone,
        Starlight and autumn and rain,
I rinse it with tears from my rupturing eye,
        Washing and making me clean.

Dear God, be more wary of all that you send,
        Sunlight and summer and sun,
All stumbling and beating and twitching alive,
                  Twitching alive,
For it takes forever, you know, just to mend,
        Starlight and autumn and rain,
The self for the self, with never a wife
        Washing and making me clean.

All errors accepting, you let me be born,
        Sunlight and summer and sun.
How long till it end! It is troublesome hard,
                  Troublesome hard,
To thread the dark thickets of neighboring scorn,
        Starlight and autumn and rain,
With only a prayer for the blackest reward
        Washing and making me clean.

When I'm five years under then dig in my ground,
    Sunlight and summer and sun,
And tenderly scrape me all off in the wind,
        Off in the wind,
Then put me all back, for my bones are sound,
    Starlight and autumn and rain,
With a ghost of a blessing to you from Poor Will,
    Washing and making me clean.

Desperate Equations

Without sex,
Little energy;

Little energy,
Small value;

Small value,
Poor pride;

Poor pride,
Useless grace;

Useless grace,
No redemption;

No redemption,
No loss;

No loss,
No philosophy;

No philosophy,
No subject.

I bring you greetings,
Warmly human:

Woman to man,
Man to woman.

Crane

One day when childhood tumbled the spongy tufts
Banking the naked edge of our bottomlands
A shadowy sand-hill crane
Arose from Rocky Spring with a flipping fish,
A speckled rainbow,
Speared in her slim black bill.
She offered her wings in sluggish waves,
Wading impossibly up the slapping waters,
And ascended the crystal floods.

Under that dark ark
Two grappling anchors of dangling legs
Rolled away so smoothly the eye forgot them
Until that tall ungainly crane
Lay in the sky like a dream.
Her snaking head
Pivoted vaguely over our deep, green valley
And straightened to kiss the horizon.
Fish and crane
Swam through the white bowl of blue air,
Spinning outward upon
Mountainous heights and their soft mysterious pulleys.

My naked shoulders ached for the tumbling clouds,
And my shivering legs
Thrashed through those mossy fishing meadows,
Over the rose-pebbled bottoms,
And churned in the chilled and iridescent spawn
Of the crane's pool.

Clamped and flexed in the vise of her beating wings
Now flaring astride the brassy eye of the sun,
I gasped like a fish
Hung out in the harsh and sudden air
And flipped, past sparkling regions, underground.

Looking Backwards in Spring
(for R. A.)

The thicket drops its autumn leaves,
 Drying its summer thorns,
And bristles in its snowy beds,
 All horns.

Well, well enough. We do without
 Until the armor cracks
And the false skeletons of love
 Fall on the axe.

Oh who can spread him as the Nile
 If on a rocky plain?
Or not come on the drouth of love
 With pain?

Invasions of a summer wood,
 Declensions of the mind,
Who can foresee the shade of good
 Trailing behind?

A Love for God

The sudden rocky rooms at waterfalls
    Contain us as we climb.
       They batter down
Our earthly aspirations, while our hearts
Leap to that haven where the water springs,
    The cool draughts of love.
       Our peace will come.

Washing with endless waters all our limbs,
    Sea, in its paler mask,
       Entices us.
We sink to it; it whitens in our hair.
Fall and be loved completely while you can,
    Then rise, or slowly drown.
       Our peace will come.

Even the shades of trees invite us up
    Into a breeze of loves.
       That cave of leaves
Hides us from friends. A green weather of boughs
Tells us to search for heaven out of this,
    And the top limbs let us down.
       Our peace will come.

Shall we assault the mountains? There they stand
    Coldly awaiting us.
       We go to them.
Over luxuriant foothills body runs
Until it flees the snow in hostile heights,

Shakes once, and shivers down.
Our peace will come.

God always threatens. His love makes us bold.
It is almost too much
To touch your hands,
Extremities that fall and freeze and drown.
But though an insanity of happiness is death,
I'll go. And then come home.
Our peace will come.

Second Principles

When you say that the moss-rose harbors a juicy stem
And gathers its moisture out of the arid air
And thrives in a blazing sun, what have you said?

You have said that the object exists and is worth attention.
That you gave it attention and found it worthwhile to report
That the moss-rose under the sun has a juicy stem.

You have said that the parts of creation are many and strange,
That we follow them, one by one, in a greenwood hope
That the sum of their parts is, itself, a significant record.

You have said that the sun cannot wither this miracle dry,
And that haunted with miracles men find it useful to go
Hunting in the universe in search of their identities;

You have said that they sometimes find it among the rocks,
Nature a naked psychology under their eyes,
The ironies of cool behavior under their senses.

So coolness can come, you have said, from a crown of fire,
Water out of the sun, tenderness out of the stones.
Even dun circumstance flowers upon the world

If you are there to watch it, if you report it,
If in reporting you grant it a color of mind
And a color of language. There on the blazing rock

The moss-roses gather sweet nectar into their stems,
Rounding and waxing their leaves and blossoms of flame.
There's one! And look, there's another! Another! Another!

The Ragged Weed

The ragged weed and the imperfect flower
Speak of perfection in this world
As if they hid
Some primal law, deep in a nodule furled.

We walk among them in their casual wild
Mutations, yet their tattered blight
Shines in the eye
As though a day were but the upper night.

I wake at dawn, not asking of my sense
Perfection of the whole or part.
I trust my mind;
And mind, I trust, honors my blood-red heart.

The ragged weed and the imperfect flower
Speak of perfection. Oh, that they
Could teach my mind
The heart of darkness in the eye of day.

Split Root

From cuts and bruises
The aspen roots
Throw up new branches
In greener shoots.

I find it hard,
Yet harshly true,
To admit to a law
In such a view;

Still, on the surface
Of bitter talk
We bruise the grass
On which we walk.

And I have admired
The Judas tree,
The crown-of-thorns,
The yew's berry.

Abroad in an April
Of aspen groves,
I can choose to forget
What the mind proves

And walk through trees
In a double stance,
Alive in that balanced
Nonchalance.

The Seafarer

Newborn, the lambs stood up.
I clapped my hands.
Mother, they wobble, but they run in bands.

And while my baby brother
Slept in his crib
The yearling lambs honored the Easter rib.

Sheep in my hobbles, sheep
Bled in my yard;
Blue eyes so meek, so meek; old hands so hard.

Slow, slow, now upward crawl
From caves of the sea.
How crude a glance against divinity.

How long a walk! We broke
The ocean mist
And shuttled up the river beds, sun-kissed.

Sheep in my hobbles, sheep
Bled in my yard;
Blue eyes so meek, so meek; old hands so hard.

Hills, mountains we strode;
Then our airstride
Stepped out upon pure space, sword at our side.

Returns to the sunswept stars,
Returns to the sun.
Star eyes holy with fire! Run, sheep, run.

Sheep in my hobbles, sheep
Bled in my yard;
Blue eyes so meek, so meek; old hands so hard.

Among Olive Groves: Montepertuso

This moment keeps its marble distances,
But in those distances the olive trees
Vaguely diffuse in parables of green;
They root our silences, defend the slopes,
And back the mountain with a silver sleep.

Sunk in our teeth the olive's bitterness,
Tangy and raw, untutored in its boughs,
Puckers the sucking lips, curdles our speech
And drives such parables against the brain
As will defile it. Save that memory.

Hauled on the hearth the knotted yellow wood
Quickens a golden tongue. Under a plane
Baroquely serpentining grains emerge,
A torture of design, while on our back
Hangs excommunication like a whip

Of thorn and spear-heart leaf at one remove,
One doveflight from the world. Small distances
Transport the olive into gracefulness
Where Jesus in our gold beatitudes
Dispensed his talents with analogies.

Those leaves were green, subtle and dull and green;
They spoke of gracile otherwheres to all
Who mused among their angularities.
If chaos brought the olive to that light,
Will broken honor raise the soul at last

68

And court it from this pale solicitude?
I look for signs among the olive trees.
A greeny leaf is there, a bitter fruit,
Grey twisted limbs, strange airy attitudes,
And prophets dreaming in the ancient groves.

Choice

Anguish is what the mind
Creates when it is stung:
Bitter in choice, not kind.

And so it is that such
Gratuities of death
Or life return in touch

That a poison woodleaf hides,
Under its thorny spine,
A medicine besides;

And that a blighted shoot
May blush the lily or
Philander in its root

And blast its ruin home
Upon the chalice which
It could not quite become.

All who would disinter,
Among the brackish clay,
Some quick adventurer

Must prick the sharp world on
A steady loving eye
To learn how they have won

The needles in the yew,
The whirlwind in the sun,
The spear invading you.

Myself in You

Conscience carouses in particular,
    Conception in event;
Who thinks the thought before he knows the act
    Surely is heaven-sent.

Idea sleeps upon the summer hills,
    Dreaming events that pass
Eroded bottomlands to rise and mate
    High in the mountain grass.

I have been plangent all these many days
    In a rough lowland sea
To come, at last, day-, year- and season-spent
    On old philosophy.

Whoever taunts that rural parable
    Must ring the thought that grows
In dying reason and expiring thought:
    Wood logic of a rose.

The mountain meadows green the valley floor,
    Chill peaks the river bed;
And somewhere in old religions of the mind
    The loin begets the head.

See, we are tinkling simples till the rude
    Simplicities extol
Myself in you; then we may both carouse
    The idea of the soul.

The Amalfi Grotto

Water is light. It blooms from dipping oars
    In huge lilies with golden tongues
        Echoing in green caves,
           A lost home.
Even stalactites sing of sudden jewels
    Dropping from bright eyes.

Just for a moment, let us dispel this charm.
The sun plunged down far undersea
Enters this cave, reflects,
Surprising us
Upon these emerald waters. Filtered light
Illuminates this world.

We cup our hands among the waves of light.
    We drip a quick florescence from
        Our watery fingers. Bells
           Ring from our arms.
The fleeting ghost of daylight everywhere
    Taps on the bone of night.

I walked on water in a field of light
    And heard the dark tides of the world
        Tell, with a bell of tongues,
           The inland sea.
I do not tell you all. But who can be
    Complete with miracles?

Naples

The bright blue bell of the sea
Blares in sulphurous sound
Rising under the city,
Trumpeting over the ground.

Yellow brass mirages
Of evangelical sun
Funnel across the haze
Of lavender waters, run

Flaring over the gulf
Through a dusty flange of song.
Thousands of crying flutes
Hurry white day long:

Traders jangle their stalls,
Assault the air with hands;
Fisheyes rot in the bay;
Smells flow over the sands;

Children charge from walls
Chalked with their buoyant signs;
Windows gape at the sky
Tangled in rags and vines.

And always, impossible sun
Hurdles the bay and rims
Steaming galleys of light
With fabulous synonyms,

Until the incredible dusk
Strolls from its violet cones
And stars roll out of the sea,
Sparkling over the stones.

Pruners: Conca di Marini

Pruners have come again among the vineyards;
They ride the terraced mountain on their ladders
To clip the grapevines hanging in these arbors.
    I heard their winter shears
    Go cleanly by these stairs.

Among the wild disorder of our twigs
Over the outer edges, frugal snips
Devour half the vines, and willow slips
    Bind up the bloodless stems
    In greys and gold reds.

Someone must train the vines (no spring has come)
Trying a few pale tendrils in the air;
Now they are clean, stripped to a winter stare.
    In less becoming more,
    Consider what is lost.

This shock will keep the vines asleep till March.
They would not dare affront their keeper's eyes
Though he is full of wine, in nothing wise
    Except these ritual chores,
    Economy of words.

For who would let a senseless love of sun
Updraw him, or a warm unseasonal rain,
Only to gaze at winter once again?
    The mild unsparing grooms
    Keep the essential roots

And pile the clippings on their women's backs
To ride the hearths and ovens of these hills
Where food and wine and fire have their wills,
    And the rank autumn grapes
    Rise in their winter flames.

Catharsis

The mossy breath of woods
Held in a tent of air
The purest solitudes;

Nothing of foul despair,
Nothing of sad alas,
Ran down the autumn there.

Petal and leaf and grass
Faded and fell, uncut,
Upon that old impasse.

Down went the bettle's hut,
The earthworm's undertow;
Then all the earth went shut

Under the sweeping snow.
King Death stood up in a bush,
Its white chills all aglow.

He shivered the spiney hush
Under his frozen hood
Until, in a secret rush,

The bleak world understood
The heart of its greener moods
And rose in the underwood.

Schweitzer

When Albert Schweitzer plays Johann Sebastian Bach
On his zinc-lined organ in Equatorial Africa,
The jungle evening cries in a carol of birds.
      (When the heart's eye is true
      Spirit will worship you.)
His healing fingers announce the preludes and fugues,
And broken arpeggios ring; then birds respond
In miniature oratorios, while their black throats
      (Obscenities they learned
      In the wild garden, spurned)
Shake the bright chain of echoes over their homes.
They come from broad-bladed palms, where primitive shades
Sleep and brood in their wings and rainbowing plumes
      (Aisles they, feinting, run
      Teaching them into the sun),
And sing, being ignorant, the only songs they know:
Flights of chaconnes, masses, and passacaglias
Wheezing from pumping bellows to whistling mouths
      (That swooping passion grown
      Toward pilgrimaging tone).
Hearing praise, they praise by instinct. Crown on crown
Of improbable song wheels over their music master;
They mimic all keys in a chaos of shrill chorales.
      (Antiphonal with games,
      Their organs pipe his names.)
It is evening, the birds at their mass. The pagan sky
In a rose of paradise gathers its feathered saints,
Vibrating their tiny flutes in thousands of throats

        (Redeemed in the simple bliss
        Of innocent artifice),
Skillfully chanting. Deep in that day-breeding dusk,
Oh, when this man is dead, let us say that he taught
The unwieldiest birds of the jungle the music of Bach
        (Making man imagine men's
        Pride in their sad amens),
Where, wide on the rim of this world, we mask that face
Fugue-flying, patiently following, putting in place
The darkening souls of earth with amazing grace.

When Swans Discover

When the snake-descended swan
Nesting in leaves blood-red
Discovers the year is gone,
He unbends his lovely head

And shouts among old reeds,
Driven, at last, to sing
Of how compassion feeds
On our diminishing,

Then sails upon a small
Abstraction of the sea
To face what might befall
His insularity.

Alone, he pauses on
A mirror of demurs
And vaguely sees the frost
In crystal rapiers

Ascending to his breast,
Descending from the skies,
Until it strike and press
A film upon his eyes.

He puffs his ragged down
Against that silver vise
And floats, a ghostly crown,
Above the threats of ice;

And then, at last, is heard
The shivering of his breath
Screaming one joyous word
Beyond the deaths of death.

Wyoming

An inquisition of the inland gulls,
That late snow masquerade upon the hills,
This leafy consonance along the draws
Conspire with the sagebrush of the ground
To blur the tongues and tempers of our house.

Here comes a man out walking in that browse,
Making, in all that space, a tiny sound.
No humid fragrance rots upon his course.
Into his eyes the blinding mountain spills
And furs his teeth with mumbled syllables.

A prism of chilled air along the limb,
Huge wild impersonal daylight in the land,
Old lizards slept upon the lava's tongue
Flow down upon us from the snow corrals
Into the heart's own meadow, saying, "Live!"

Saying that if we will, and if we live,
Some pardon waters all the dry canals
And in crisp grasses reproduces young.
Man is not welcome; he must understand
How to be welcomed though God threatens him.

A mile between the contours of each face,
Cool singleness of one and one and one,
The arching monasteries of the skies
Blossom around us in the lonely vast
Lagunal lakes of time. Oh, take my hand!

It is as though a crowd—oh, take my hand!—
Of lovers through a watered valley passed
And jeweled the next hill with their gentle eyes
To name this stranger, having come upon
A young child walking toward them out of space,
Hiding, with newborn hands, its wrinkled face.

A Wintry Meditation

Rumors of old mortality,
  The whitened head-drifts
Settle across our eyes. They blur.
  The solid landscape shifts.

Throughout the day the blowing snow
  Made bleak and sudden starts
Until the breathing chimney tongues
  Expired from our hearts.

We had been reading history,
  But the archaic page
Crumpled under our eyes and made
  A geologic age;

Our future stood in a broken range,
  Jagged upon the air;
The heart exploded in pale dusts
  And bled white everywhere.

Dust descended in riverine chills,
  Bleaching siberian space,
And petrified the minute expanse
  Of our historic face.

Then over that tundra the great Ob
  Broke on the Arctic sound
And, mute with our immortality,
  Swept northward, underground.

Hounds

Catastrophes beyond our true renown
Conscript us out of heaven till we stand
Embattled in our customs, going down.

Imagine thought among immediate fires
Like some antique philosophers; perhaps
Honor's the strange summation of desires.

It may be so. That is our living curse:
To learn, unsteadily, how lean we come
Down to the level ripeness of the hearse.

I stand against that coming, though my share
Of every passion track my honor there.

The Brothers Karamazov

Ivan: *Miracle*

All world is not enough.
Each heart is dumb;
Therefore, the mind invents
A kingdom, come.

Mystery

Clear though the sun of day,
It falls, a blight
Upon the sacred wood.
We ask for night.

Authority

And, pathless as a plain,
We understand
Only enough to say,
Sir, take my hand.

Alyosha: *Love*

Hangs love upon our hearts,
Heavy as loss?
Yes, nailed against our sky,
Kissed to the cross.

Buchenwald, Near Weimar

Through barbed-wire enclosures,
Their bodies bloodless under metallic thorns
Like an unauthorized crucifixion,
The animal faces of handsome Europe steered
And grinned and begged and leered.

They had piled some bodies up,
Naked to God, like cordwood for a fire.
If eyes and faces turned,
Or jaws hung out among the shriveled limbs,
They sang, thank God, no hymns.

Pallid with black dishonor,
Nailed to the numerals of striped uniforms,
Stripped of their native hair,
They snared me with their unashamed display
And mocked at my dismay.

A rapid frantic babbling
I took for a Slavic tongue, a complete stranger,
But a wrinkled skeleton
Wavered up the wire and whispered in English,
His mind is sick. In anguish

The proud white brow of man,
Where the eye nobly shines, had crashed down.
It groveled on the ground,
More than Greece falling, more than Rome
Razed in its charred home.

The low grey barracks stood
Dumb, in a chained line, in the torn-up land.
The bleak doggy eyes
Rolled to and fro, compounded with despair,
Blind to the exit there.

I could not touch them; I could
Not ask forgiveness, not even comfort them.
I came from another land
And stood at the deathbed of my own father again
In that vast mad graveyard of falling men.

A Magi Ballad: 1961

Old shades of man in autumn woods
　　Steal on our snow-white mare;
They mount and fly like foliage;
　　They sashay through the air.

They toll a long supremacy,
　　Gallop the gilded hills;
They thunder past our battlements
　　Of spring and summer wills.

Blazing the tournament of leaves
　　Over our cultured lawn,
Stripping the ragged ghost of truth,
　　Circling, and fleeing on,

They cry, unsheltered, at our sheds
　　And charge and charge again
To drive the fable from the woods,
　　Scales from the eyes of men.

Those shadowy riders haunt the dusk;
　　Down native nights they run
To charter our pale white cerements
　　In graves of orient sun.

Stoned, bronzed, in ancient images,
　　They pace primeval stones
With spectral visions, though they sleep
　　In darkling skeletons;

And up from a troubled dream, the race
   Imagines God and comes
In awesome journeys through blinding snows
   Like rainbows to our homes.

Upon Hearing Three Hundred Children Singing

in Jonathan Edwards' Church,
Northampton, 5 March, 1961

I heard three hundred children singing sweetly together,
Cleanly in robes, their bright eyes looking at heaven,
And their voices floating out of their innocent faces
Under the nave. High under the chancel windows
They met the rainbowing sun, and they sang together.

I heard three hundred children marching along together
With hearts all gay and their shapely mouths all smiling,
And over and under and through them the great bass organ
Ground out processional laws in the modes of their sermons,
Delivered in chorus before all their mothers and fathers.

Three hundred children, all singing under those shadows,
Admonished the devil, and all in the clearest soprano
Roaming the vales of our tears with a jubilant leisure
Under the stern director. But under the shadows
The pipes blew faintly in forests beyond their meadows.

Hearing three hundred children singing so sweetly together
I remembered that once I was singing, so many together,
And the sanctifications were lost in a fable of Sundays
And fabulous Mondays; and yet I was glad to be chanting
In such casual guises as now I am nevermore singing.

I heard three hundred children ascending the hymns and
        carols

While fathers and mothers sat in their dark rows, smiling,
And thought: how delightful, innocent, charming and proper
It is for our children to sing, who must walk through shadows
And the long long valleys upward to mothers and fathers.

I heard three hundred children communing at decorous altars.
I forget what they sang (maybe something as glossy as morals)
But their faces shone in their songs, and I dreamt that evils
Foregathered among them and stalked around in their
   singing,
But still they sang on to sons and their sons' generations.

I heard three hundred children wound in the wisdom of ages
And all of them cheery about the dark words they were
   chanting,
Yet clever enough for their words. Oh, their minds so clearly
Moved with the music and sun I forgot they were singing,
Being father and son and grandson and greatgrandfather

Hearing three hundred children at play in the heavenly
   chancels
And three hundred children at song in the blossoming
   meadows
And Adam at morning out walking with Eve by the apples.

A Chide Against Self-Pity

Time passing, harried and graceless,
    Tramps like a nervous scarecrow
Into the bedrooms of another morning.
    He glares

Hard at the sleepy vagrancies of sense
    And flaps the down comforters
Loose. In that blue unheated air
    Five icicles

Riffle our necks with goosepimples;
    The gape of chilly truth
Maddeningly follows, follows, follows.
    Dear God,

If we had not gathered our wits and risen
    More than ten thousand times
We might have been lying there, scared stiff,
    Still.

Tree on Slope, Snow on Stone

Beating it with the old stick of poetry,
I hobbled an awkward word along
Into an old song.

Caned with polished ivory,
It fled into another country
Until we came to a solemn landscape
Lit up through scrolls of angular distortions
And split bamboos
Into a silken screen.
There, a humped man and crumpled donkey
Struggled off to a corner of southern valley
And leaned in the broken shade
Of splayed reeds.

Far, far to the north
The gods in their absolute mountains
Rose in the sunstruck afternoon
In monuments of silent attitudes
And balanced, tree on slope,
Snow on stone.

Pull up that ragged coat around your ears,
Old man;
Cover that shaggy donkey with a spear
Of prayers in crooked hands.
This is the artist's home.
Let the ice come.

Recollection of Octobers

Nature is half asleep in ponderous trees,
Trees in the leaves, the leaves blown in the sky
And the sky in a wet commotion for the fall

When all the leaves fall down upon that breast,
Sodden as heavy mothers. I climb the limbs,
Childlike among the children of this earth.

God, what a day! It sings with a skip and swing
And a blue dream blossoming over the highest bough;
Hunger and sleep will down me soon enough

To send me crunching home, over the leaves
That yesterday blew down, over the leaves
Today blew down, blew down, over the leaves,

Until my grace notes hang on a staff of twigs
And frost cracks up and sky flakes slowly down
And nature is sound asleep in ponderous trees,

Like music, asleep. Sleep is a music, too.
How, on a winter night, muffled in sleep,
Blackbirds sing in their red wings over the streams

Breaking under the snow. Now all night long
Old autumn days come on, and as they come
Sun plays over the leaves, leaves under the sun.

Rock

Observed from age to age,
The water's arrogance
Stabs at the earth, a rage
Of damned munificence.

Spun from the ocean plains
Clear to its polar caps,
Who knows what world it drains,
What country takes? Perhaps

It lures and smiles and lies
Beyond our sandy sweeps;
Yet, seen with ageless eyes,
Whole armies from its deeps

Rise on our shores and crash
Over our walls. One hears
Only that single clash
Joined for a million years.

If patience were a rock,
Anger the pounding sea,
I should prefer to mock
That mad intensity;

And though I, grain by grain,
Fail in those fluid wars,
I still might entertain
Such thundering visitors

As long as one could shout,
As far as one could hear,
Until the earth give out
Or judgment reappear.

Thirteen Poems
From The Green Town

POETS OF TODAY III

Willows

Willows are trees of life. They ride
Their limp boughs to their feeding ground
And sound
Their roots in their immediate countryside.

Like them, I, too, survive
By circular and seasonal disguise;
One golden childhood willow kept my eyes
In a huge green honey hive;

Those twigs and saplings of indifferent dreams
Blooming upon their mountain meadowlands
Sprang in my hands
Like shadows on the upper willow streams.

Now down they run like water to broad plumes
Of delta beds
And toss their palaces of tangled heads
In green felicities of trailing rooms

While rivers in the silted sands dispute,
With sea-borne gravity,
The overflowing tree,
The plunging siphon root.

That thirst would drink the creek beds dry:
Or so I thought. But minnow schools
Sparkle in willow pools,
Shifting their golden flecks in that bright eye.

So have I lain in depths while vision pearled
Over the clouded surfaces of things
In dense imaginings
With one eye squinting upward into the world

Out of my willowy sleep. That memory calls
Where the old willow tells
Of disembodied cities of floating bells
Tumbling simultaneously through waterfalls.

The spring floods flash. Believe me, one can not
Casually remember now
All jewels hidden under the willow bough,
In all-begetting time what one begot.

When I am an old man and dying, almost lost
On the northern slopes of death, a stiff reed
Trembling from husk to seed,
My flutes all cracked with frost,

I will translate myself into a brown
Paradise of willow roots, a whole
Country of mountain meadows for the soul
Dreaming toward natural grace in a green town.

The Serpent

The hooded reptile, in his guile,
Knows how to dance and how to smile.

Some say he merely writhes and grins
Through solemn subtleties of sins,

But look, his jeweled body turns
To rings and bracelets in the ferns.

He grazes on the velvet grasses
With coral feet, then dewlike passes

Flickering on the darkling ground
In neural sandals of no sound.

Glimpsed at the lily pool, he glides
Serene among its undertides

And wakes soft ripples into bells
Of water sepulchered in shells;

So kissed, he resurrects his head
Above the broad-leafed lily bed

And blasts the ivory blooms among
Pale whispered powders of his tongue.

Standing in water like a spring
Long-coiled for Satan's underling,

Spinning through subterranean loves,
Feeding upon pure lily groves,

He makes an ikon with his thin
Needle of spiraled medicine.

Seductive, convoluted, poised,
He equals elements, unvoiced

Except for one hushed song of death,
A sudden exodus of breath.

And now he floats and slides and soars,
Glistening upon the further shores

And waves toward Calvary, his gloss
All intersected in a cross;

Depending from our lidded eyes,
Lovely upon that flesh, he lies,

There, hung in haloes, all amazed,
So slyly caught, so subtly praised,

Fleeing among his purple stings
Love dances, smiles. Oh, how he sings!

Ecclesiastes

Out of the icy storms the white hare came
Shivering into a haven of human arms;
It was not love but fear that made him tame.

He lay in the arms of love, having no name
But comfort to address. Shaking alarms
Out of the icy storms, the white hare came

Across the haunted meadows crackling with fame.
What evil eye pinpointed his soft charms?
It was not love but fear. That made him tame

Among the chilling hail and scattering aim.
Helpless against the sport of ancient farms,
Out of the icy storms the white hare came

Thinking, perhaps, it leaped through icy flame,
Thinking, with instinct, hate or trust disarms.
It was not love. But fear that made him tame

Leaped again in his heart; his flesh became
Translated into havens. From sudden harms
Out of the icy storms the white hare came;
It was not love but fear that made him tame.

Market Street Elementary School

Here, at the child-cry of morning,
Embrace the bright rope-skippers on the walk
Singing at games
Under the wiser eyes of immobile nuns.
> Jump in the circle,
> Polly and Joe,
> With one little foot
> And one big toe.
Nineteen-twenty—the circling chorus
Sings inviolate numbers, while metronomes
Beat in double strands blending through their slow whirl.
> Swing in the circle,
> Polly come Sue,
> With two little feet
> And big toes too.
Can this be April, Alice, Bright Abstraction
Gracing centripetal whirlwinds of delight?
Swirled in rhythms of twenty-nine thirty
She moves in axioms and hypotheses
Proved for an instant.
Thirty-nine forty—what ancient choir
Circled the amphitheater of mind
With such melodious precision?
> Who shall we dance for?
> Dance for the Queen:
> The prettiest lady
> You ever have seen.
Radius shrinks and wavers, but figure keeps
The planes of purity; bouncing, she skips

Through awesome forty and nine,
Hearing the clapping hands
Of impatient adolescence and design.
      If you have a sharp eye
      Watch how the rope goes
      Or, abacadabra,
      You'll fall on your nose.
Brutal as Mother Goose and the Brothers Grimm
(The nuns impassively acknowledge
The world from which they fled)
The twirlers, accelerando, wink
Between their numberings. Fifty-nine sixty.
Witch has made her sign.
World spins.
And loud unlovely choric voices guess
Who next will leap to the blurred parabola
When Blue Innocence
Trips out of music and geometry
And falls to earth, her airy lightness gone,
Tangled in hemp and human dissonance.

Henri Matisse

Discrimination through pure color
Is one sure way to shock
New admirations from the universal heart.

Anaphoras of sound, another.
And proud angular lines
Circling upon the dancing of their own rhythms.

If blue ladies sleep on a green couch
In a green room, dreaming
Beyond yellow roses and pink blinds to the clear

Blue Mediterranean, dreaming
As far as eyes can dream
Beyond those bedroom windows, then one red petal

Flicks on the mirrors of the sea,
A floating miracle
Flaming upon that subtle and watery world

And all clear. We were, you know, in dreams:
Blue ladies somnolent,
Yellow roses in vases silent as roses—

And then, psst, Monsieur Henri Matisse
Looked at his world and said,
I'm lonely, and in his own image created

The green ennui of Eden, mild blue
Skies, and sleeping ladies
Arousing their blue heads under his apple boughs.

War

When my young brother was killed
By a mute and dusty shell in the thorny brush
Crowning the boulders of the Villa Verde Trail
On the island of Luzon,

I laid my whole dry body down,
Dropping my face like a stone in a green park
On the east banks of the Rhine;

On an airstrip skirting the Seine
His sergeant brother sat like a stick in his barracks
While cracks of fading sunlight
Caged the dusty air;

In the rocky rolling hills west of the Mississippi
His father and mother sat in a simple Norwegian parlor
With a photograph smiling between them on the table
And their hands fallen into their laps
Like sticks and dust;

And still other brothers and sisters,
Linking their arms together,
Walked down the dusty road where once he ran
And into the deep green valley
To sit on the stony banks of the stream he loved
And let the murmuring waters
Wash over their blood-hot feet with a springing crown of tears.

A Sea-Change: For Harold

Across the swamps and marshlands of the hours,
Over the cloud-banked air and under the dark
Hills of fog where lamps
Float incandescent caves in drowsy streets,
The drowned sound of the sea wells up in foghorns
Blowing out of their watery towns.
That chilled grey groan
Rises on sunken mountains, upon
Oceanic rain-eroded shores, under
Hollow crystal gongs in icy poles,
And rides through cabled water-years of sound
To echo upward over the rusty buoys,
Bobbing and clanging in a blind mist
Along our inward bays,
To cry an old sad song in the soggy bones
Under our chalky shores.

The cold ache and dull blue sound of the sea
Fades in the foaming crests,
Whispers at rocks,
Jutting their grey-green heads from the grey-green sea,
And sleeps in the world's great valleys.
There the riding ocean sighs
Over the shoals of continental shelves
Down to submerged kingdoms
Where drowned soldiers, logged in the sound,
Dream that their salt-encrusted eyes
Glow in the weeds and corals of their skulls.

Across broad rivered deltas and crumbling cliffs
That long grey sound
Faintly vibrates over the ocean floor
And rises under our surface solitudes
As if a huge volcano, muffled under the sea,
Erupted with no sound.

Dry Grass

The hayfield whispers as I walk
Each midnight hour up this hill
To tell the autumn wind such talk
And nonsense as I will.
I mark the sumac by the moon
And tear the withered grass to show
How crisp stems crackle, and how soon
The searching fingers know
Beyond old callouses and tough
Thin tentacles of nerve that this
Is death again.
                  I like that rough
Sharp certainty that is
Portion of hand and part of mind.
For if, sometimes, I run in fear,
Bewildered, questioning and blind,
At least I have death here,
Real in my human hand. It
Is reassuring, being clean
And common to my autumn wit
And in my memory, green.

Fall of Icarus: Brueghel

Flashing through falling sunlight
A frantic late plunging from its strange
Communicating moment
Flutters in shadowy waves.

Close by those shattered waters—
The spray, no doubt, struck shore—
One dreamless shepherd and his old sheep dog
Define outrageous patience
Propped on staff and haunches,
Intent on nothing, backs bowed against the sea,
While the slow flocks of sheep gnaw on the grass-thin coast.
Crouched in crimson homespun an indifferent peasant
Guides his blunt plow through graveled ground,
Cutting flat furrows hugging this hump of land.
One partridge sits immobile on its bough
Watching a Flemish fisherman pursue
Fish in the darkening bay;
Their stillness mocks rude ripples rising and circling in.

Yet that was a stunning greeting
For any old angler, peasant, or the grand ship's captain,
Though sent by a mere boy
Bewildered in the gravitational air,
Flashing his wild white arms at the impassive sea-drowned
     sun.

Now only coastal winds
Ruffle the partridge feathers,

Muting the soft ripping of sheep cropping,
The heavy whisper
Of furrows falling, chip cleaving,
Water lapping.

Lulled in the loose furl and hum of infamous folly,
Darkly, how silently, the cold sea suckles him.

Hunters in the Snow: Brueghel

Quail and rabbit hunters with tawny hounds,
Shadowless, out of late afternoon
Trudge toward the neutral evening of indeterminate form.
Done with their blood-annunciated day
Public dogs and all the passionless mongrels
Through deep snow
Trail their deliberate masters
Descending from the upper village home in hovering light.
Sooty lamps
Glow in the stone-carved kitchens.

This is the fabulous hour of shape and form
When Flemish children are grey-black-olive
And green-dark-brown
Scattered and skating informal figures
On the mill ice pond.
Moving in stillness
A hunched dame struggles with her bundled sticks,
Letting her evening's comfort cudgel her
While she, like jug or wheel, like a wagon cart
Walked by lazy oxen along the old snowlanes,
Creeps and crunches down the dusky street.

High in the fire-red dooryard
Half unhitched the sign of the Inn
Hangs in wind
Tipped to the pitch of the roof.
Near it anonymous parents and peasant girl,
Living like proverbs carved in the alehouse walls,

Gather the country evening into their arms
And lean to the glowing flames.

Now in the dimming distance fades
The other village; across the valley
Imperturbable Flemish cliffs and crags
Vaguely advance, close in, loom,
Lost in nearness. Now
The night-black raven perched in branching boughs
Opens its early wing and slipping out
Above the grey-green valley
Weaves a net of slumber over the snow-capped homes.
And now the church, and then the walls and roofs
Of all the little houses are become
Close kin to shadow with small lantern eyes.
And now the bird of evening
With shadows streaming down from its gliding wings
Circles the neighboring hills
Of Hertogenbosch, Brabant.

Darkness stalks the hunters,
Slowly sliding down,
Falling in beating rings and soft diagonals.
Lodged in the vague vast valley the village sleeps.

Ever Green

Over the forest stones
Old evergreens arise in pyramids
    Of everlasting summer
    Crowned in burnished cones.

Gold in their haloes climb
These green geometries, bright byzantines
    In the blue apse of God.
    Poised in its paradigm,

Each evergreen appears
Spired upon our dark horizon. Night
    Shatters daily upon
    Their million greeny spears.

Up from their misty glades
They rise upon the world and prick our thoughts
    To miracles and rainbows,
    Sunlit among shades.

Supple in wind, they thrust
Up toward the winter sun through shining frost;
    All boughs arise like flags
    Blown from their nets of dust.

Under the snow's descent
From branch to weeping branch, the waving boughs
    Crystal with fragrance make
    A comfortable tent;

117

In that green cone I lie
Warm in reflective arms, while icicles
Mirror the outer boughs,
Jewel the inward eye.

Let all their greenness keep
Some cool and wintry attitudes, that still
No winds or fire may sweep
Such comforts from our sleep.

A Little Homily for the Holy Seasons
of the Spirit

Through all my childhood I
Often beheld ragged sparrows
Flying upward throughout a series of lesser fallings,
Beating their filmy feathers against the nest-clogged barn
      eaves.
Being no St. Francis feeding
Among the field lilies,

I fell through tumbling air.
It is scarcely daring for birds
To begin falling; then grace is natural. Bedazzling
Flight begins in descent until lovelier upswinging
Embraces the side-slipping winds.
Then birds fly and heart skips.

Descent is good folly;
Therefore, it is sometimes holy
Inasmuch as bird-natural worlds are an expression,
In ranges of goodness and omnipresent wickedness,
Of bright platonic otherworlds
And omnipotent wills.

Think how young hummingbirds
Flutter out from motherworld homes
While birdsmall bones, immaculately curving and hollowed,
Find that the air is home and all flight hallowed orisons.
History makes orioles, doves,
Swallows saintly. And gulls,

Though sung briefly. Gaze by
The twirling life-span of God's birds.
One sees them battered by windshields of your bishop's Buick,
Pounced on by amoral cats, shocked by boy-triggered rifles,
Frozen through hungers unto death,
Poisoned for plagues of filth

In the human cities.
Oh, from any open window
Bede's sad and fleeting sparrow, Shelleyan larks, the rough
    ark's
Dove, the militant eagle, penguins of Anatole France
Flee past spiritual atolls
Of a priori soul

Into birdlike islands.
Though divine illusion insists
That natural flight is holiness, it is no such thing;
We ascend to destruction and fall to the realms of grace.
But if all birds fell from the air
Imagine our despair.

Imagine orioles
Spinning their orange flames toward earth,
Millions of barn swallows not rising out of their dipping,
Odd birds of paradise falling out of their paradise
Heavy as stones and dipped arrows,
And hosts of dead sparrows.

Imagine all soaring
Fieldlarks now silently falling,
Even the parrots and guinea hens ceasing their squawking,
Water ouzels not singing, every bald eagle fallen,
Sandpipers and rosy grossbeaks,
Shrikes, canaries and teals

All falling. Imagine
These feathery constellations
Tumbling on snowpeaks, on green plains and turquoise sea
    waters,
Cardinals, goldfinches, wrens, bluebirds falling from graces,
These rainbowing appellations
All falling. Imagine!

And silently falling!
Even the raucous crows, alas,
And saw-winged buzzards silent, magpies, camp-robbers, blue
    jays,
Bobwhites, owls, nuthatches, blackbirds! How would you like
    to see
The mourning dove making no moan
And the phoenix a stone?

And all the gulls plunging
Down into waves forevermore
In deathly congregations? And bright mothlike humming-
    birds
Crushed in canterbury chalices? The olive-white dove,
Despite all heaven's commotions,
Lost in endless oceans?

Oh, it is neither good
Nor evil that troubles us here,
But rather spiritual affinities. I have now
Spoken of ascension, resurrection and death. In you
They all lodge in disguises of
Holy and profane love.

Winter Juniper

Above these bleak Wyoming plains,
These high plateaus
Where water seldom rises through the rock,
This twisting cedar grows.
Splitting through sharp and sandy grains
Of buried cliffs, its fragrant seedlings mock
Deep humus soils and rains.

Under a bright December sun
This cedar pricks
With waxed and polished stems the arid air,
Pivots angular sticks,
Quivers in western winds; they run
Through and away. Here with such final care
Its tortured life is done,

And done, and done again, until
The grained wood
Spirals into a balance, a defense,
A grace. One night I stood
Under the moon in a midnight chill,
Caught in that alien axis, grown immense
In that green will.